THE HUNDRED GRASSES

LEILA WILSON

THE HUNDRED GRASSES

POEMS

milkweed
editions

Published 2013 by Milkweed Editions
Printed in the United States
Cover design by Hopkins/Baumann
Cover art by Lewis Knauss
Author photo © John W. Sisson, Jr.
13 14 15 16 17   5 4 3 2 1
First Edition

Milkweed Editions, an independent nonprofit publisher, gratefully acknowledges sustaining
support from the Bush Foundation; the Patrick and Aimee Butler Foundation; the Dougherty
Family Foundation; the Jerome Foundation; the Lindquist & Vennum Foundation; the
McKnight Foundation; the voters of Minnesota through a Minnesota State Arts Board
Operating Support grant, thanks to a legislative appropriation from the arts and cultural
heritage fund; the National Endowment for the Arts; the Target Foundation; and other
generous contributions from foundations, corporations, and individuals. For a full listing of
Milkweed Editions supporters, please visit www.milkweed.org.

Library of Congress Cataloging-in-Publication Data

Wilson, Leila.
 [Poems. Selections]
 The hundred grasses : poems / Leila Wilson. -- First edition.
   pages cm
 ISBN 978-1-57131-447-5
 I. Title.
 PS3623.I585485H86 2013
 811'.6--dc23

                              2012037158

Milkweed Editions is committed to ecological stewardship. We strive to align our book
production practices with this principle, and to reduce the impact of our operations in
the environment. We are a member of the Green Press Initiative, a nonprofit coalition of
publishers, manufacturers, and authors working to protect the world's endangered forests and
conserve natural resources. *The Hundred Grasses* was printed on acid-free 30% postconsumer-
waste paper by Edwards Brothers, Inc.

For my mom, who showed me place.

For my dad, who taught me space.

Table of Contents

In the four directions, broad plain on plain;
east wind shakes the hundred grasses.
—Eastern Han Dynasty, 25–220 A.D.

THE HUNDRED GRASSES

What Is the Field?

The field is filled
with what we see
without sleep.
Never completely
closed, it quickly erodes
when tilled before rain.

If clogged with boulders
it won't be razed
and once burdened
cannot quicken
under flocks.

The field reveals
glint and holds
leaning, pulls
twist from taut
knots of buds.

We watch the field
for stirring, wait
for stems to spring
back from sparrows.

We hope for a swell
in its middle so
we can say we saw
the sway that comes
from noticing.

Water meanders
to prairie potholes,
throws cordgrass
into switchbacks
as we push past
bramble and scare
a whistling wheel
of geese into air.

The field draws
hawks and sides
of trains, cradles
pools from storms
where ducks plumb
for water snails.

We trample light
between us,
no way to lope
in parting the swales.
We must flatten
to fill the space

with all the rolling
wrapped up in us.

Before home,
the gabled barn
across the road
throws the brightest
rise we've ever seen
the field try on.

The field is not
in rows, is not
a faded saw-songed
croon. It pushes green
a mist above mud,
shows how we make do.

We wonder
what we're not
in the field.
What scours, cuts,
or knocks.
If we could stay
and still feel full
the low line rounding
out a spread
of subtle slope.

Nether

*The equilibrium of any particular aspect of
nature rests on the equivalence of its opposites.*
—Piet Mondrian

Some land lives
so water can comb

it into grids. This
is why lowlands

tilt still toward
the sea. This so

we call our canal
leaning horse,

hat tempting wind,
somewhere a tear

in linen where
the loom bent

a heddle. We plant
lapis in the middle

of begonia boxes
hung from our

houseboat's sills.
At night the eels

snug against
our houseboat's hum,

water's warm hem.
We hear them slip

itch into our floor.
Our houseboat lilts

when the bigger boats
slide us waves.

Our concrete floats.
We're mostly moored

to stay. In the damp
bank where the ducks

hedge weeds,
our bikes sleep.

We lean toward wind.
Our pant legs thin

from all the rain
on our knees.

From here the horizon
gauzes above us.

We are half hidden
by light. We are folds

in fog. We stand
open on the deck

and beckon the silt
to settle. We wait

for a balance so grand
that any flicker

of inverse could
pull us up to spires.

Air Parts

I.

Whenever weight
shifts, a hollow
rouses in its pith.

Egg's air. Door
hinge oiling for rain.
Her hush as

the truck jolts.
All mass enfolds
gaps. All wind

and fury when a tree
litters light through
her window screen.

She wants to know
how she'll go down
unraveling.

II.

There's nothing
hallowed
in a ferry's quake

before it slips
toward sinking.
Full of its last

owned move,
it will be a hole
in the bay.

It will hold air
and bleed perforations.
After bedding,

it will be pilfered
by those who want
emptiness to touch.

III.

Outlined by shadow
or echo or that
which happens after,

mosquitoes trace
her with tremble.
Her hand holds

off rain, a herd
beyond the hill.
Her swallow's

salamander grove
skids in thin wind.
How her voice scratches

from calling names,
how her neck strains
past straightening.

IV.

Because the sky
can't fill all in,
and ceremony

comes nowhere
near, she looks
for something else

to pull her pulse.
Balconied gasp.
Bubble riding

the river's leg.
Cracks. Lesions.
Mesh. She traps

the inside until it cores
there. She mills
the middle stillness.

Hedge // Yellow Field

What weeds
as an explanation
leaves out, is
that chaos
is not our condition.
—Charles Olson

When imagining
a field not there,
or this one

shuttered
behind blunt
branches, yellow

pushes through
from a brow
all bent with birds.

Wanting swallows
to still, to stay
themselves

on sways of wire,
leaves making time
strain meaning

from the quiver
they slur and float.
This one patch

of land I can't frame
with fingers, but
I work my gaze

to keep it mine.
My eyes clamor to
help it rise

into fervor—
roughly hewn
figure—that could

yoke and drag,
drawing my path
black toward

its weedy center.
The hedge hems in
the nearest knowing

I'll never see.
It breaks in
me the lapse

that brought
me here. Tangle that
clings to far air.

Branches

Like stairs
they depend

on angles,
creaks uncoiling

from every cramp.
They hook heat.

They save rain.
Their knuckles

sap at dark,
blot dirt,

the ground's mane.
They are best seen

bare in their
struggle, or ours.

There is no
fixed distance.

Beneath the Overpass

Each car carries
its own shivering.
Each litter of silos
a suddenness
from field.

* * *

We see a man
skidding rocks
down the slant
cement
inside this land's
one hill.
He knows
the swept moment,
where sound
collides with view.

* * *

Sun sidles
its stretch on tracks
at dusk.

The man says
that ramulose
weed is brush.

He fills in crops
with dust
and brings luck
back to rocks he
cracked it from.

* * *

The barn lamps
yellow his face:
*If you could go
where I lived, you'd
meet the woman
who left me water
when I wanted
at pasture's edge.*

* * *

We can tell in him
how houses hold
their doors toward
distance.

As from a train
some fields fray

along the creeks
where children
pitch their sacks,

while other fields
get threshed
too soon and crack
in winded snow.

* * *

I was a wanderer.
Then the king
of debugging. I used
to filch peaches
going through French
Lick. That was over
by the river when
the river was rich.

* * *

When storms shake
open a rush
of hair, he says
he likes the wires
straining away
from here. Part
city, part lace.

In September
trucks thicken
and hit the monarchs
flitting south.

* * *

He'll hold watch
he says: *I'll hold*
watch until night
when animals
cling to bark
and children
fall asleep in cars
that brush along
back roads.

In turns the dreamers'
breathing circles
bodies as they soften.
A wheel bleached
by stars, a wheel
that swells in sleep,
it keeps on
swallowing ground.

Ancestral

Oat dust roiled
beneath the muzzle. Hands
swabbed the saddle.
The only fix for hooves

was lime rind stewed
with lard then drizzled
into nettles.

Middelharnis
not so far from Bethel.
When mine dammed back
the sea, they waited for break.

When yours pushed
lake through a hole,
they sluiced a stream.

Someone saw in dusk
a bat or a swallow.
In brine by the bank
some mallow.

Someone saw the girl
he should have loved run past.
Someone feared the devil.

Yet when they rode,
all rode toward us.
Sun stinking in the hay
stuffed back in the stable.

The sky in their hair caught
in scrambles. Coattails, skirt hems
snagged by bramble.

Spur rust trailing
thin pleats from home,
they trotted on their failing.
They bet on us mid-stride.

And before they died
they heard the ridges
of their room softened

by children scraping
floor boards. Their car wheels
small exhales shifting
vroom, vroom, vroom.

Character Architecture

Bodies, being
built from

other bodies
aren't built

of light. So
when I see

a shadow
crouching in

my building's
crux, it's natural

I think
that it could be

a bachelor.
I don't want

to be scared
into going back

to the same bed.
No one else has

come to me like
this: has sprung

my mind's moth,
opening

eyed wings.
I am ready for

a room dethorned
of chairs, where

I could forge
my whole refrain

on open floor.
Where I could be

dreamed by a blue
soldier, shining in

the windows' way,
spindling into place.

Back Spot Turn

I have felt her in this house,
The blond bride, who long languished here.
—Rainer Maria Rilke

Even in the angle
of the way I wake,

I quarry the air
with breaths I rend

from it. A table
braces my water

glass, my gown a tangle
at my feet, a vane

clicking in the wind
outside. What brides

lay here past morning,
wasp nests ago,

grass lifting blaze above
bloated seed heads?

They must have heard
the milk-can handle

drop against
its metal shoulder,

must have touched
the skin beneath

their eyes with ice.
Yesterday my dress

was all strum
leaning into night,

all chalk on fingers
walking across a desk.

I felt them watch
for my second guess.

I did not let my hem
snag planks.

I danced and shed
my father's name.

What thud there was
was close to toes.

What happenstance
was grown at home.

What dark
didn't dissolve

in the green air
of caught bugs

clung to the flush,
the preened hand's breeze.

Bed Brightening

(After Les Murray)

I wanted us to talk
with the sudden snaps

of carbonation
misting at our lips.

I wanted you to see
sky snagging trees,

tamping beetles into
shade, how night

after night ribbed
wings flung off dew.

My jeans are weighed
with fingered rocks

and acorn hats and
pulled-out springs.

Oh, Orpheus—
you never got to feel

cold air on my heel
or hear slow

joints of trains
jolted awake

by clasping
down-track cars.

The shift of light
or quick knock

into life that
radios make before

they play songs.
These clicks shoot

off in the drawers
by my bed. Glasses

chime in sinks nearby.
Rabbit ears tauten

with motorcycle
throttle just out

of range to guests.
But every ear

is a broken bowl
held back together

with fissures exposed.
My room corners

curve. Dust seeps
into grooves.

I am my own
kind of static.

Lisp of Cloud

The fog, a flock, thickened
the field. Steps

bereft of stepping's stay.
So goes my trilled

bone's shiver, more
release from land

than river. My hold
a sip of snow

caught in a crater.
I am new to you

in this light. In touch,
a garden blond

with wandering water.
I am scattered in

this exhale I imagine
as flight. Not dust or fact,

skin or dawn. This world
skews away,

limning. Branches
both shadow and spinning.

Farnsworth House

My whole house
means that I may
stretch out along
lines of the river.
Hinges hidden,
counter taut,
ottoman lifted
just above the floor.
Windows pull length,
here the expanse
of the thin white
roof horizon
tamping down
its open bones.

I loved the man
who wanted me
seen by the earliest
specs of green
come spring.
He wanted me
leaning into

the brightest side
of stone, constant
flow toward home.

I know this river
covers an inner-
quaver, the quick
shifts of animals
moving away,
damp smell
hunching in holes.

It catches color
of pin oak bark.
It glares then waxes,
dawning me in
reeds, blanching
me with light.

Shining a crack
in land, my fate
unfolds along
these banks: cool
marble planes
float me just above
this mud and tint
my legs with glow,
a glued hum
beneath my gown.

All things bulge
in throats and clots.
Inside I dry;
I lie supine
and watch
for water's roil
to nip the trees
at their wet stems.

He's been gone
for years,
and I hear worms
thumb into the tug
toward river.
All the seeping
and suction,
scales and branches
slurring with frogs,
their weight grazing
the laden ground.

A rivet by
the river's crook,
I gauge the water
streaks it sheds.
If fish, ever fast
beneath my feet,
slick the grass
that knows the wind

against its sides,
then I, in my
pock of air will
ride the current
free, hung here.

Anniversary

Your phoebe arrives,
sprays loose dew

into a hem
along the hill.

My breathing caught
and filled, sudden

surge of wind.
The fence cramped

with sawed-off
branches straining

toward the road.
A wrist gone

bad from sowing
seeds. My love

halved past happening.
Lingering sprawled

to swell. I would
again rise to fall,

choose to have you
here to head away.

Ocean Inn

Once
to shed our din,
to slip into
a coastal wake,
we come again
to find a thrall
further out
from us now:
a swell that falls
back into its brink,
a baby who
wills its rift
from body before
any air
can worry it.
Waves quit
the horizon
to find us sloughed
off the dunes.
They shoulder,
they quiver,
unfolding fog
to stream.

They pull back
and bleed aspects
of what we want
to still:
pipers' legs
that punctuate
insect break,
or footfall flaring
out our weight
through sand.
We are sails that flap
on land; we well
with place.
We are bound
to ground
and to the lace
the foam leaves.

Sail Dilation

Always tending
toward,
first half
      prolonged
of a yawn.

Lake
      and line
that tamps
it back.

In the middle
      a quiver,
body axles,
      cleaving
      wind.

The boat
could slip
      into a sway
      beyond the eye,

the body blown into.
      Waves could keep
      their collapse
from shore.

      Then this sail
loosen
its clutch
      on air
and fray.

There's no hinge
      to flapping,
no vastness when
a fish litters
      the still
      with swash.

A long look
      ebbs all soft hope
      eventually.

A spine of posts
      trickles

from land's
thicket stand.

You can't hold
        splendor
in a squint.

You can't sand
    a view
    so bent.

III

Pocket Compass

I. North

That winter
    children born
        in the bright room

by the town's
    caught train saw
        past the damp field

to know a color
    dented in ground:
        held frost of downed corn

II. South

Shallow cradle
of palm
A girl

balls up a frond
until she sees
the spin

in veins wound
tight beyond
all frill

III. East

Geese glide
   over the flat
      school roof

They tell the boy
   who muses far
      too much in class

how gutter water
   gleams a river
      soon to ice

IV. West

Opened
    the cave wall
        sheds shadows

Where stones
    bead glint
        ground clutches

Here people still
    want to sleep
        and touch hands

Tributaries

This kind
of wet air
is not how
I know
myself as clear.

Yet blur
is how my face
feels best.
Thin river
shaped to mud.

Water smear
of mallard
lunge. Stretched
stems hanging
over boulders

hedging shore.
Oregon river
sung before by
men with paddles
carved to cattails.

My Illinois
stream is still
unnamed, sliver
from a plane.
Slipper for a girl

who's tripped again
by branches on
her way to cup
a flock of bugs.
Bean swill

caught in beetle
brush. Small
barrage of stones
clinging near
the bank for good.

My smooth water
steams untethered
from a lake,
no glacial nudge.
It carries leaving

on its back.
It carries
hawk tail feathers
and buries glass
broken in the barn.

Not big, cows
drink from it.
Not shy, I know
the light
its blinking throws.

Pond Song

I felt the pond
near when I heard

a horn playing there.
I was cooking by a window

next to squirrels
shaking leaves.

Streetlamps burned
the screens blue.

A bike's gears
itched by below.

In the living room
my love darned

sock toes. Sparing
stove flames'

brittle hissing rush,
no danger hooked here.

Nothing shouldered
or severe when a sound

from the pond broke
through. I had heard

it before at the end
of a hall's open ear:

a bassoon poured forth
a boy's first breath

through the reed.
Mouth sore with air.

An ache I didn't know
tone could strain

from me out loud.
It meant my brother

could come back.
It meant the water

might have bled
for sound like thaw,

that pain—quelled
lean—could spread.

With mist holding
homed light open,

no better feeling
to know what's wrong

when blare marked *far*
clings close to here.

The Solent

(After Whistler)

Wind sleeps creased
inside the channel

Water another glyph
toward distant canter

These sooty boats bring
birds with moons
in their feathers
        minds huddled
and peels askew

Sheets hang over
and sometimes sails
unbind   pale chime
of lanterns hung
along the moored

No boats holy
sodden at shore
yet this one's
lapse is air   is far
from here where

lights it left still skim
among chords

where lights it left still
trickle and curl

Promise   a river
that's leaving land
brimming to
cloudscape whorl

Promontory

The day I lost
your face

to a rocky edge
or distance,

lakeshore
suddenly cluttered,

the loon flew.
Its head wended

down. And bark
knotted moons

it knew. All blown,
the waves mawed

for your mouth.
No other touch

was worth
the stretch.

Knees left pocks
in clots of mud.

Air bunched
thrown light

into fog.
Bodied only

by moving.
Water kept

curling the cast-
out back in.

Lawn Archaeology

I did not think over
the bone's curve

buried and grown.
I did not mow

its inside split until
the fence unhemmed.

Hill's cursive length,
edge of gnawed field.

Fault was mine and land
drained down its crawl.

Sweet pea cove
a bottom curl.

Gaunt glint,
an inkling whistled

through. What got cut
was blank, was white

sewn into blue.
When it shook open,

hope hummed
ground. Domed

not dead. Nest
and crown drawn new.

Wisconsin Rubbing

Purple clover
flowers measure
mist on the hillside's
over-sloping
shadow. Small
fingers mat
grass. *What wind,*
people say. What
elastic thronging
fills the field where
no one has died.
Longing seals
a man with leaving
he knows he will
choose, cool as
a snout, more breath
than stream.

Driftless Region

In this chair
on the hill
I'm higher than
the house below,
chaparral
lacing its beams.

* * *

I'm the biggest
animal here,
and so little hair.
Vines hurl
themselves at me.

* * *

A branch beside
loosens from a tree.
Its bark, too,
slackens from
branch, cloaking
a slit for bats.

* * *

I've been here
trying to trace
clovers' spasms
and as they dry,
their dying.

All summer
they've held up
hovering of bees,
chaffed down by
practiced sound,
the hum a boy
holds in his mouth
on an afternoon floor.

* * *

The phone tower
bulbs across the field,
filled with drivers'
murmurs stretching
out toward towns.
The river sidles
then slips away.
Windshields flash
with leaning light.

Inside the blush
the sky throws
swelling, how can
I capture scatter,
fold into passing,
my breathing
flocked with flaw?

Tracing Her Frolic

Because milkweed
seeds in wind
I learn to bend,

I snag the pause
in arch and vine,
in caves
and hanging song.

I reach the throat
where river wobbles.
I lip-read leaves
thrown out to drown.

Wherever little
balls rolled tight
between these greener
fingers reach.

Rustle unveils
room bunched
inside summer's skin.

The thrush throws bare
an arc of air, caught
beneath a branch's wing.

The fence starts
behind the fronds.
I'm large
beyond my face.

Shade falls low,
a crux, a nape
for fog, or fog.

IV

Span

Within its pause,
the core of a deer.

Around the body
hairs sharpen light.

At home,
a pock of loss
in the center.

A warbler
as long as my thumb
draws cottonwood
around its song,
seeds floating
into linden waft.

The soft stomach
of home
and warmth
between the eyes.

Mist cast
in the marsh
beyond
the drawn bushes

holds the moon
grazing reed tips
by the Galien,
the highway-nicked
raccoon.

The deer shocks twigs
behind the thicket.

While chewing,
we wait to watch
each other stretch,
how we dismantle
food from crown.

To think
of moving back
traps the flight
of bugs between us.

We brace for the blur
the curdling
suddenness makes.

Small lights
in the room
suckle corners.

Clicks within
the breather
net the bed,

clicks within roots
fill the mouth.

Outside the deer's
swallow rolls down
her neck's curve.
As if trying on shoes,
she steps,
divots in mud.

This morning a wood
thrush hit the glass, left
red blots in a clutch.
They could
have been berries
from up the walk,
the beak an open clamp.

While straining
to hear
the kettle's boil,
the bird's body.

What is the name
for a beak tap
buried by impact,
feathers blunt
and tinged?

Dying done, I turned.
Light slatted
and stretched on the floor.

After daisies dry,
their fists held
at passersby.

What was there
to notice before?

The room smelled
of bark.
In flight
some finches fall
then fall again.

Though latched
to burrow
and always by water,
the woodchuck airs
land for the beaver.

Caterpillars colonizing
the pagoda dogwood
pulse together in their tent.

Home is molded
by the way I move.

A terra cotta pot
struck by a crack
holds the last
plant's prints.

My hands
thistle over my body
in the cold store.

The food I press
sticks behind its skin.

The door screen's
small squares
spill how I stare.

Soon
white spots
led from fawns
through fall
will trail
sallow sun.

When still,
some mammals
see long
swathes of space
curtained by sheets
stomaching gusts.

What mimicry
of gardens can I
gather in rooms?

What of wind
does skin admit?

In the lull
between clotheslines
slack with rain,
the flies hang sheen
over the yard.

Inside, light only
from holes.

Certain curves
recur around
our bodies
and then in
animals at rest.

I thought I could
lean against death
longer.

Wind wraps
poppies closed
so seeds won't scatter
all together.

I don't know
what to do
with love
left over.

Through tree break,
lichen grows
below the sound
of wind
or inside the sound
of deer.

Echoes in scratches,
breathing's
last letting
still traces
the throat.

A grackle's shadow
flickers over my face;
a mosquito
nears my lashes.

Absence is not
an opposite.

Night stewed
with lamplight
around a house
presses back
as something else.

The toad's slow
pulse draws him
toward the door
flung with bugs,
and when he's gone
I step around
where he watched.

I can adorn
the dead, cluster
phlox by ribs
where too much air
kept food from
filling in.

After the pause
around the body pulls,

I try to feel
a far turn.

I hold
rolled paper
and hear steps
echo in my palm,

left to crop
what I can
from this copse.

Acknowledgments

I am grateful to the editors of the following some in slightly different form: *American Letters & Commentary, Canary, Court Green, CutBank, Delmar, The Iowa Review, LVNG, MoonLit, Poetry,* and *A Public Space.*

I am also grateful to the Poetry Foundation, Lake Forest Academy, and the Roger Brown Faculty Enrichment Residency of the School of the Art Institute of Chicago for financial support and writing time.

I have deep gratitude for Shirley Stephenson and Dan Beachy-Quick for their generous engagement with this book over many years. Thanks to Allison Wigen and Daniel Slager at Milkweed for their vision and stewardship, and to Wayne Miller for his critical eye. Many thanks to the friends who supported these poems along the way: Averill Curdy, Josh Kotin, Nicolette Bond, Miranda Johnson, Chicu Reddy, Suzanne Buffam, Robyn Schiff, and Nick Twemlow.

Most pronouncedly, thanks to Peter Thomas.

Leila Wilson was born and raised in DeKalb, Illinois. She teaches at the School of the Art Institute and University of Chicago. A former editor at *Chicago Review*, she is the recipient of a Friends of Literature Prize from the Poetry Foundation. She lives with her husband and son in Chicago.

Interior design and typesetting by Hopkins / Baumann
Typeset in Adobe Caslon Pro